D1379443

Tarsiers
in the Dark

By Thomas Van Eck

 **Gareth Stevens**
Publishing

Please visit our website, www.garethstevens.com. For a free color catalog of all our high-quality books, call toll free 1-800-542-2595 or fax 1-877-542-2596.

Library of Congress Cataloging-in-Publication Data

Eck, Thomas Van.
Tarsiers in the dark / Thomas Van Eck.
p. cm. — (Creatures of the night)
Includes index.
ISBN 978-1-4339-6382-7 (pbk.)
ISBN 978-1-4339-6383-4 (6-pack)
ISBN 978-1-4339-6380-3 (library binding)
1. Tarsiers—Juvenile literature. 2. Nocturnal animals—Juvenile literature. I. Title.
QL737.P965E35 2012
591.5'18—dc23

2011036078

First Edition

Published in 2013 by
Gareth Stevens Publishing
111 East 14th Street, Suite 349
New York, NY 10003

Copyright © 2013 Gareth Stevens Publishing

Designer: Daniel Hosek
Editor: Therese Shea

Photo credits: Cover, p. 1 Masterfile.com; pp. 5, 7, 9, 13, 19 Shutterstock.com; p. 11 Priit Vesilind/National Geographic/Getty Images; pp. 15, 17 iStockphoto.com; p. 21 Jay Directo/AFP/Getty Images.

Printed in the United States of America

CPSIA compliance information: Batch #CW12GS: For further information contact Gareth Stevens, New York, New York at 1-800-542-2595.

Contents

Boldface words appear in the glossary.

Big Eyes, Big Ears

Imagine walking through the dark, wet forests of Southeast Asia. Suddenly, you see an animal that looks a bit like a monkey with very large eyes! It's a tarsier (TAHR-see-uhr). Tarsiers are **primates**, just like monkeys, apes, and humans.

5

A tarsier has a flat face and round head. Its eyes are very large for its little body. It can't move its eyes. It has to turn its head. However, tarsiers can turn their head almost all the way around!

7

Tarsiers' large eyes help them see well, even in the dark. They have large ears, too. They can hear very well. Tarsiers can open and close their ears. Tarsiers' ears are always moving except when these animals are sleeping.

9

On the Move

When tarsiers want to move, they leap from tree to tree. Their strong back legs push them forward. They can jump as far as 20 feet (6 m)! When tarsiers are on the ground, they hop on their back legs.

11

Tarsiers have pads on their fingers and toes that help them hold on to tree branches. Their long, thin tail has hair at the end of it. They use their tail almost like another arm or leg.

13

Midnight Snacks

Tarsiers are **nocturnal**. They sleep in trees during the day. At night, they look for food. Their large eyes and ears help them. Tarsiers mostly eat bugs. They eat spiders, lizards, and birds, too.

Baby Tarsiers

Tarsier mothers usually have one baby at a time. The baby is born with fur, and its eyes are open. Tarsier babies start leaping when they're only a month old! They can catch their own food after 2 months.

17

Where Are the Tarsiers?

Tarsiers once lived many places around the world. Today, tarsiers are **endangered**. They only live in a few places in Southeast Asia. People have hunted tarsiers for food and cut down their forest homes.

19

There aren't many tarsiers left today. Some people have tried to make them pets. Tarsiers hate to be in cages. They may even hurt themselves trying to get out. People need to **protect** these animals in their wild homes!

The Tarsier Fact Box

Length	body, 3 to 6 inches (8 to 15 cm); tail, 5 to 11 inches (13 to 28 cm)
Weight	about 4 ounces (113 g)
Where They're Found	Southeast Asia
What They Eat	birds, bugs, lizards, and spiders

Glossary

endangered: in danger of dying out

nocturnal: active at night

primate: any animal from the group that includes humans, apes, and monkeys

protect: to guard

For More Information

Books

Hoare, Ben. *Endangered Animals*. New York, NY: DK Publishing, 2010.

Stefoff, Rebecca. *The Primate Order*. New York, NY: Marshall Cavendish Benchmark, 2006.

Websites

Philippine Tarsier
animaldiversity.ummz.umich.edu/site/accounts/information/Tarsius_syrichta.html/
Read much more about tarsiers, including how they talk to each other.

Philippine Tarsier Foundation
www.tarsierfoundation.org
Find out how people are working to save tarsiers in the Philippines.

Tarsiers
nature.ca/notebooks/english/estars.htm
Read more facts about tarsiers, and see photos of them in trees.

Index